TABLE OF CON

Chapter 1

Introduction

The concept of self-esteem lies at the heart of human psychology, influencing the way individuals perceive themselves, their capabilities, and their place in the world. It forms the foundation upon which personal growth, resilience, and well-being are built. Self-esteem is not a static attribute; rather, it is a dynamic and evolving aspect of one's identity that requires conscious nurturing and development. At its core, self-esteem encompasses a profound understanding of oneself, a deep appreciation of one's worth, and the ability to navigate life's challenges with confidence and authenticity.

In this exploration, we delve into the six pillars of self-esteem, a comprehensive framework that encompasses the key principles and practices necessary for fostering a strong and healthy sense of self-worth. These pillars—Living Consciously, Self-Acceptance, Self-Responsibility, Living Purposefully, Personal Integrity, and Building Trust/Credibility—form an interconnected system that contributes to the holistic development of self-esteem. By understanding and implementing each pillar, individuals can embark on a transformative journey of self-discovery, personal empowerment, and meaningful fulfillment.

Throughout this discussion, we will delve into the intricacies of each pillar, examining their significance, practical applications, and the ways in which they intersect to create a powerful foundation for self-esteem. We will also explore common obstacles that can impede the cultivation of self-esteem and provide valuable techniques to overcome self-doubt and setbacks. As we navigate this exploration, it becomes evident that self-esteem is not merely a destination but a lifelong endeavor—a continuous process of growth, reflection, and self-improvement.

Join us as we embark on a comprehensive journey through the six pillars of self-esteem, uncovering the tools and insights that can empower individuals to cultivate a robust and resilient sense of self-worth. Through the integration of these principles into daily life, one can unlock the potential for authenticity, purposeful living, and a heightened appreciation of one's unique qualities. The journey toward enhanced self-esteem is a testament to the profound impact of self-discovery and personal development, offering the promise of a more empowered and fulfilling existence.

Importance of self-esteem

Self-esteem refers to the overall assessment, value, and perception an individual holds about themselves. It is a fundamental aspect of psychological well-being that plays a crucial role in shaping how people think, feel, and behave. The importance of self-esteem cannot be overstated, as it influences various aspects of an individual's life, from their mental and emotional health to their relationships, achievements, and overall quality of life.

Emotional Well-being: A healthy level of self-esteem contributes to positive emotional states such as happiness, contentment, and inner peace. When individuals have a positive self-image and believe in their abilities, they are more likely to experience lower levels of anxiety, depression, and stress.

Resilience: People with higher self-esteem tend to be more resilient in the face of challenges and setbacks. They are better equipped to cope with adversity and are more likely to view challenges as opportunities for growth rather than insurmountable obstacles.

Motivation and Achievement: Self-esteem plays a significant role in motivating individuals to set and pursue goals. When people believe in their capabilities, they are more likely to strive for success, work harder, and persevere in the face of obstacles. Positive self-esteem fuels a sense of efficacy and confidence, leading to increased achievements.

Healthy Relationships: Healthy self-esteem is essential for forming and maintaining healthy relationships. Individuals with a positive self-concept are more likely to engage in respectful and fulfilling relationships. They set and maintain boundaries, communicate effectively, and avoid toxic dynamics.

Decision-Making: Self-esteem influences decision-making by guiding individuals to make choices aligned with their values and aspirations. People with higher self-esteem are more likely to make assertive decisions that support their well-being rather than succumbing to peer pressure or seeking external validation.

Physical Health: Studies suggest a link between self-esteem and physical health. Positive self-esteem is associated with adopting healthier lifestyles, making better dietary choices, engaging in regular exercise, and seeking medical care when needed.

Creativity and Innovation: Individuals with healthy self-esteem are often more open to exploring new ideas and taking creative risks. They are not as constrained by fear of failure and are more likely to think outside the box, leading to increased innovation.

Conflict Resolution: People with self-esteem are better equipped to handle conflicts constructively. They can express their needs and concerns assertively while respecting the views of others, leading to more effective conflict resolution.

Job Performance: Positive self-esteem can impact job satisfaction and performance. Employees who value themselves are more likely to feel competent and capable in their roles, leading to improved job performance and greater career success.

Overall Life Satisfaction: Ultimately, a healthy self-esteem contributes to an individual's overall life satisfaction. When people feel good about themselves and their abilities, they are more likely to experience a sense of fulfillment, happiness, and a positive outlook on life.

In conclusion, self-esteem is a foundational aspect of human psychology that profoundly influences various facets of life. Cultivating a healthy self-esteem is a lifelong process that involves self-awareness, self-acceptance, and continuous self-improvement. By recognizing and valuing one's worth, individuals can lead more fulfilling lives and contribute positively to their own well-being and the well-being of those around them.

Chapter 2

THE SIX PILLARS OF SELF ESTEEM

Pillar 1: *The Practice of Living Consciously*

Living consciously is a fundamental pillar of self-esteem that involves being fully present and engaged in one's life, choices, and experiences. It encompasses self-awareness, mindfulness, and taking responsibility for one's actions. This practice is essential for fostering a healthy sense of self-esteem and well-being. Let's delve into the detailed explanation of this pillar:

Self-Awareness: Living consciously begins with self-awareness – the ability to observe and understand one's thoughts, emotions, behaviors, and reactions. It involves introspection and a willingness to explore one's inner landscape. Self-awareness helps individuals identify their strengths, weaknesses, values, and beliefs, which are essential components of a healthy self-concept.

Mindfulness: Mindfulness is the practice of being fully present in the moment without judgment. It involves paying attention to thoughts, feelings, sensations, and the surrounding environment. Mindfulness encourages individuals to observe their experiences without getting caught up in automatic reactions or distractions. This practice cultivates a sense of clarity, focus, and emotional regulation.

Accepting Responsibility: Living consciously also entails taking responsibility for one's choices, actions, and outcomes. This involves recognizing that individuals have agency and control over their decisions. Accepting responsibility empowers individuals to make intentional choices aligned with their values and aspirations, rather than reacting impulsively or blaming external factors.

Engagement: Living consciously encourages active engagement in daily activities. Instead of going through the motions or operating on autopilot, individuals consciously invest their attention and energy in what they do. This fosters a sense of purpose, satisfaction, and meaning in both mundane and significant tasks.

Authenticity: Embracing conscious living allows individuals to express their authentic selves. When people are mindful of their values and desires, they are more likely to make choices that reflect who they truly are, rather than conforming to external expectations or pressures.

Reducing Regret: By practicing conscious living, individuals can minimize regrets. They make decisions with greater awareness, considering the potential consequences before taking action. This proactive approach reduces the likelihood of making impulsive choices that may lead to later regrets.

Emotional Regulation: Living consciously supports emotional regulation by enabling individuals to observe their emotions without becoming overwhelmed by them. Mindful awareness allows for a more measured response to emotional triggers, reducing impulsivity and promoting emotional well-being.

Quality Relationships: Being fully present in interactions with others enhances the quality of relationships. Active listening, empathy, and genuine connection are all fostered through conscious engagement, contributing to healthier and more fulfilling social connections.

Personal Growth: Practicing conscious living facilitates personal growth and self-improvement. By being aware of one's thoughts, behaviors, and challenges, individuals can identify areas for development and actively work towards positive change.

Enhanced Well-Being: Ultimately, the practice of living consciously contributes to enhanced overall well-being. It supports mental, emotional, and even physical health by promoting self-awareness, reducing stress, and fostering a sense of control and agency.

In conclusion, the first pillar of self-esteem, the Practice of Living Consciously, encourages individuals to be fully present, self-aware, and responsible in their lives. By cultivating mindfulness, embracing authenticity, and making intentional choices, individuals can lay a strong foundation for a healthy sense of self-esteem and a more fulfilling, meaningful life.

Self-awareness and mindfulness

Self-awareness and mindfulness are two essential components of the Practice of Living Consciously, which is one of the six pillars of self-esteem. These concepts are closely related and play a significant role in fostering a strong sense of self-esteem and well-being. Let's explore each of them in detail:

Self-Awareness:
Self-awareness is the foundation of conscious living. It refers to the ability to recognize and understand one's own thoughts, emotions, behaviors, strengths, weaknesses, values, and beliefs. It involves looking inward and gaining insight into one's inner

world. Self-awareness is a multidimensional process that encompasses various aspects:

Emotional Self-Awareness: This involves recognizing and understanding one's emotions, including their triggers and impact on thoughts and behaviors. It allows individuals to differentiate between different emotions and develop emotional intelligence.

Cognitive Self-Awareness: Cognitive self-awareness involves being aware of one's thought patterns, beliefs, and cognitive biases. It helps individuals identify self-limiting beliefs and negative self-talk, enabling them to challenge and reframe these patterns.

Physical Self-Awareness: Being attuned to physical sensations and bodily reactions helps individuals understand how their body responds to different situations and emotions. This awareness can contribute to stress reduction and overall well-being.

Social Self-Awareness: Understanding how one interacts with others, including communication styles, interpersonal dynamics, and social cues, enhances the quality of relationships and social interactions.

Benefits of Self-Awareness:

Personal Growth: Self-awareness is a catalyst for personal growth and self-improvement. By understanding their strengths and areas for development, individuals can actively work towards becoming the best version of themselves.

Enhanced Decision-Making: Self-aware individuals make more informed decisions because they consider their values, emotions, and cognitive processes. This leads to choices that align with their goals and aspirations.

Effective Communication: Self-awareness enhances communication skills by enabling individuals to express themselves clearly and understand the perspectives of others.

Stress Management: Being aware of emotions and stress triggers allows individuals to manage stress more effectively and develop coping strategies.

Healthy Relationships: Self-awareness contributes to healthier relationships by fostering empathy, understanding, and effective conflict resolution.

Mindfulness:

Mindfulness is the practice of being fully present and engaged in the present moment without judgment. It involves directing one's attention to the here and now, observing thoughts, emotions, sensations, and the environment with curiosity and acceptance. Key aspects of mindfulness include:

Non-Judgment: Mindfulness involves observing experiences without labeling them as good or bad. This non-judgmental awareness promotes self-compassion and reduces self-criticism.

Curiosity: Mindfulness encourages a sense of curiosity and openness to one's experiences, even if they are uncomfortable or challenging. This attitude supports self-discovery and learning.

Acceptance: Mindfulness involves accepting the present moment as it is, without trying to change or control it. This acceptance leads to reduced resistance and greater emotional resilience.

Benefits of Mindfulness:

Stress Reduction: Mindfulness practices, such as meditation and deep breathing, are effective tools for reducing stress and promoting relaxation.

Emotional Regulation: Mindfulness helps individuals become more aware of their emotions and respond to them in a balanced and constructive manner.

Improved Focus and Concentration: Regular mindfulness practice enhances the ability to concentrate and stay focused on tasks, leading to increased productivity.

Enhanced Well-Being: Mindfulness is associated with greater life satisfaction, positive emotions, and overall psychological well-being.

Reduced Rumination: Mindfulness reduces rumination – the repetitive and unproductive thinking patterns that can contribute to anxiety and depression.

In summary, self-awareness and mindfulness are interconnected practices that contribute to the Practice of Living Consciously. By cultivating self-awareness and practicing mindfulness, individuals can develop a deeper understanding of themselves, manage their emotions more effectively, make intentional choices, and experience greater well-being and self-esteem.

Being present in daily activities

Being present in daily activities, often referred to as mindfulness in action, is a vital aspect of the Practice of Living Consciously, one of the six pillars of self-esteem. It involves focusing your attention on the task at hand and fully immersing yourself in the present moment. This practice brings numerous benefits to your mental, emotional, and overall well-being. Here's a detailed explanation of being present in daily activities:

Understanding Being Present:

Being present means directing your awareness to your current activity, whether it's a routine task, a work assignment, or a leisure activity. It involves engaging all your senses and focusing on the details of what you are doing, rather than getting lost in thoughts about the past or future.

Key Elements of Being Present:

Full Engagement: When you are present, you are fully engaged in the activity without distractions or multitasking. You give your complete attention to what you're doing, allowing you to perform tasks more effectively and efficiently.

Sensory Awareness: Being present involves using your senses to experience the moment. You notice the sights, sounds, textures, tastes, and smells associated with the activity, enhancing your overall sensory experience.

Open Curiosity: Approach each task with curiosity and an open mind. This mindset encourages you to explore new perspectives and find joy in even the simplest activities.

Non-Judgment: Being present also means observing without judgment. You refrain from labeling experiences as good or bad, allowing you to accept things as they are and reducing unnecessary stress or negativity.

Benefits of Being Present:

Reduced Stress: Being present helps alleviate stress by diverting your focus away from worrisome thoughts. When you fully engage in an activity, you create a mental break from stressors.

Enhanced Focus and Productivity: When you give your undivided attention to a task, your focus improves, leading to increased productivity and better results.

Improved Relationships: Being present in interactions fosters effective communication and connection. People feel valued and heard when you engage with them fully.

Mindful Eating: Paying attention to the taste, texture, and aroma of your food can lead to healthier eating habits and a more enjoyable dining experience.

Emotional Regulation: Being present allows you to observe your emotions without getting swept away by them. This self-awareness helps manage emotional reactions more skillfully.

Mindful Living: Engaging in daily activities mindfully can lead to an overall sense of mindful living, where you appreciate the small moments and find joy in everyday experiences.

Practical Tips for Being Present:

Single-Tasking: Focus on one task at a time and resist the urge to multitask.

Breathing Awareness: Use your breath as an anchor to bring your attention back to the present whenever your mind starts to wander.

Mindful Transitions: Pay attention during transitions between activities, such as walking from one room to another or shifting from work to leisure.

Digital Detox: Dedicate time without electronic devices to fully engage in activities and connect with your surroundings.

Practice Mindfulness: Engage in formal mindfulness practices, such as meditation, to train your mind to stay present.

In conclusion, being present in daily activities is a powerful practice that enhances your well-being, improves your relationships, and contributes to a deeper sense of self-esteem. By incorporating mindfulness into your daily routine, you can experience greater satisfaction, reduced stress, and a more enriched life.

Accepting responsibility for one's choices

Accepting responsibility for one's choices is a crucial aspect of the Practice of Living Consciously, one of the six pillars of self-esteem. It involves acknowledging and owning the decisions you make and their consequences, both positive and negative. This practice plays a significant role in personal growth, self-accountability, and cultivating a healthy sense of self-esteem. Here's a detailed explanation of accepting responsibility for one's choices:

Understanding Responsibility:
Taking responsibility means recognizing that you are the author of your choices and actions. It involves acknowledging that your decisions influence your life outcomes and affect those around you. Responsibility is not about blame but about accountability and empowerment.

Key Elements of Accepting Responsibility:

Ownership: Accepting responsibility requires owning up to your decisions, without making excuses or shifting blame onto external factors.

Consequences: Recognizing that every choice has consequences, both intended and unintended, is a fundamental part of responsibility. This includes acknowledging positive outcomes as well as addressing challenges.

Learning: Embracing responsibility involves a willingness to learn from your choices, whether they lead to success or failure. This mindset promotes personal growth and development.

Self-Awareness: Being aware of your motivations, values, and beliefs helps you make informed decisions aligned with your authentic self.

Proactive Mindset: Accepting responsibility encourages a proactive approach to life. Instead of feeling like a victim of circumstances, you take charge of your choices and work towards desired outcomes.

Benefits of Accepting Responsibility:

Personal Growth: Taking responsibility fosters self-awareness and a willingness to learn from mistakes. This promotes personal growth and leads to continuous self-improvement.

Empowerment: Acknowledging your role in shaping your life empowers you to make deliberate choices that align with your goals and values.

Improved Decision-Making: Responsibility encourages thoughtful decision-making as you consider the potential consequences of your actions.

Enhanced Relationships: Accepting responsibility fosters trust and respect in relationships, as others see you as reliable and accountable.

Reduced Stress: Owning your decisions reduces stress by eliminating the need to rationalize or make excuses.

Resilience: Accepting responsibility helps you bounce back from setbacks with a sense of purpose, as you view challenges as opportunities for growth.

Practical Steps to Accept Responsibility:

Reflect: Take time to reflect on your choices and their outcomes. Acknowledge what went well and what could have been done differently.

Avoid Blame: Instead of blaming external factors, focus on your own actions and decisions when assessing a situation.

Apologize and Make Amends: If your choices have negatively impacted others, offer a sincere apology and take steps to make amends.

Learn from Mistakes: Embrace the lessons from your experiences, both successes and failures, to make more informed decisions in the future.

Set Goals: Define your goals and values, and make choices that align with them to create a sense of purpose and direction.

In conclusion, accepting responsibility for one's choices is a cornerstone of conscious living and self-esteem. By acknowledging your agency, learning from experiences, and making deliberate decisions, you empower yourself to lead a purposeful and fulfilling life.

Pillar 2: *The Practice of Self-Acceptance*

The Practice of Self-Acceptance is a fundamental pillar of self-esteem that involves embracing and valuing oneself unconditionally, regardless of strengths, weaknesses, and perceived flaws. It is a practice of self-love and compassion, allowing individuals to cultivate a positive self-image and a healthy sense of self-worth. Let's delve into a detailed explanation of the second pillar:

Understanding Self-Acceptance:
Self-acceptance is the practice of fully embracing who you are, without judgment or the need to be perfect. It involves acknowledging your entire self, including your physical appearance, personality traits, emotions, and past experiences. Self-acceptance is not about denying the need for self-improvement but about approaching growth from a place of love and understanding.

Key Elements of Self-Acceptance:

Unconditional Love: Self-acceptance is grounded in self-love and compassion. It involves treating yourself with the same kindness and understanding that you would offer to a friend.

Self-Compassion: Practicing self-compassion means extending understanding and forgiveness to yourself when you make mistakes or face challenges. It involves treating yourself with the same kindness you would show to others.

Embracing Imperfections: Self-acceptance means acknowledging that everyone has imperfections and recognizing that they are an integral part of being human.

Letting Go of Comparison: Comparing yourself to others can hinder self-acceptance. Letting go of comparisons allows you to appreciate your unique qualities and experiences.

Non-Judgment: Self-acceptance involves refraining from harsh self-criticism and negative self-talk. It encourages a mindset of self-kindness and understanding.

Benefits of Self-Acceptance:

Improved Mental Health: Embracing yourself with self-acceptance can reduce symptoms of anxiety, depression, and low self-esteem. It promotes a more positive and resilient mindset.

Higher Self-Esteem: Self-acceptance is closely linked to self-esteem. When you accept yourself as you are, you build a solid foundation for healthy self-worth and confidence.

Enhanced Relationships: Self-acceptance allows you to show up authentically in relationships, leading to deeper connections and more genuine interactions.

Stress Reduction: Embracing yourself with self-acceptance reduces the stress associated with unrealistic expectations and the pressure to meet external standards.

Freedom to Grow: Self-acceptance provides a safe space for personal growth. When you accept your starting point, you can more freely work towards positive change.

Resilience: Self-acceptance fosters emotional resilience, allowing you to bounce back from challenges and setbacks with greater ease.

Practical Steps to Practice Self-Acceptance:

Practice Mindfulness: Mindfulness helps you observe your thoughts and feelings without judgment, fostering self-acceptance.

Positive Affirmations: Use positive affirmations to challenge negative self-talk and reinforce self-acceptance.

Journaling: Write about your thoughts, feelings, and experiences to gain insights into your self-perception and practice self-acceptance.

Set Realistic Expectations: Set achievable goals and expectations for yourself, taking into account your strengths and limitations.

Practice Self-Compassion: Treat yourself with kindness and understanding, especially in times of difficulty or self-criticism.

In conclusion, the Practice of Self-Acceptance is a powerful pillar that allows you to embrace your authentic self with love, compassion, and non-judgment. By cultivating self-acceptance, you lay the groundwork for a strong sense of self-esteem, mental well-being, and meaningful relationships.

Recognizing and embracing one's strengths and weaknesses

Recognizing and embracing one's strengths and weaknesses is a fundamental aspect of the Practice of Self-Acceptance, which is one of the six pillars of self-esteem. This practice involves understanding and appreciating your abilities and limitations, fostering a healthy self-concept, and promoting a positive sense of self-worth. Here's a detailed explanation of recognizing and embracing strengths and weaknesses:

Understanding Strengths and Weaknesses:
Strengths are your inherent or developed qualities, skills, and attributes that contribute positively to various aspects of your life. They are what you excel at and what makes you unique. Weaknesses, on the other hand, are areas where you may have limitations, challenges, or room for improvement. Recognizing both your strengths and weaknesses provides a balanced and realistic view of yourself.

Key Elements of Recognizing and Embracing:

Self-Awareness: Self-awareness is the foundation of recognizing strengths and weaknesses. It involves introspection and observation to understand your abilities, preferences, and areas where you may struggle.

Embracing Strengths: Embracing strengths means acknowledging and celebrating your accomplishments, talents, and skills. It involves taking pride in your achievements and recognizing the value you bring to different situations.

Accepting Weaknesses: Accepting weaknesses involves acknowledging areas where you may have limitations or challenges. It's about being realistic and compassionate with yourself, understanding that imperfections are a natural part of being human.

Growth Mindset: Embracing weaknesses with a growth mindset involves viewing them as opportunities for learning and improvement rather than as permanent limitations.

Benefits of Recognizing and Embracing:

Enhanced Self-Esteem: Acknowledging and appreciating your strengths boosts your self-esteem by reinforcing your sense of competence and value.

Authenticity: Embracing both strengths and weaknesses allows you to show up authentically in various situations, fostering genuine connections with others.

Improved Relationships: When you are aware of your strengths and weaknesses, you can communicate more effectively, set realistic expectations, and collaborate with others based on your abilities.

Goal Setting: Recognizing strengths helps you set achievable goals aligned with your abilities, while acknowledging weaknesses helps you identify areas for growth and development.

Resilience: Embracing weaknesses with a growth mindset builds resilience, as you approach challenges as opportunities for learning and improvement.

Practical Steps to Recognize and Embrace:

Self-Assessment: Take time to reflect on your experiences, skills, and qualities. Make a list of your strengths and areas where you may need improvement.

Seek Feedback: Ask for feedback from trusted individuals to gain insight into your strengths and areas for growth.

Positive Self-Talk: Replace negative self-talk with positive affirmations that acknowledge your strengths and encourage growth.

Set Realistic Goals: When setting goals, consider your strengths to build on and your weaknesses to address. Break down larger goals into manageable steps.

Celebrate Progress: Celebrate your achievements and milestones, both big and small, as a way of recognizing and appreciating your strengths.

In conclusion, recognizing and embracing your strengths and weaknesses is an essential practice for cultivating self-awareness, self-acceptance, and a positive self-esteem. By understanding your abilities and limitations, you can approach life with authenticity, set meaningful goals, and build a strong foundation for personal growth and well-being.

Overcoming self-criticism and negative self-talk

Overcoming self-criticism and negative self-talk is a crucial aspect of the Practice of Self-Acceptance, one of the six pillars of self-esteem. It involves changing the way you perceive and communicate with yourself, fostering self-compassion, and cultivating a more positive and nurturing internal dialogue. Here's a detailed explanation of how to overcome self-criticism and negative self-talk:

Understanding Self-Criticism and Negative Self-Talk:
Self-criticism and negative self-talk are patterns of thought that involve being overly harsh, judgmental, or critical of oneself. These inner dialogues can erode self-esteem, create unnecessary stress, and hinder personal growth. Overcoming these patterns involves shifting towards more self-compassionate and supportive ways of thinking.

Key Elements of Overcoming Self-Criticism and Negative Self-Talk:

Awareness: The first step is becoming aware of your negative self-talk patterns. Pay attention to the thoughts and messages you tell yourself, especially when faced with challenges or setbacks.

Challenge Distorted Thoughts: Often, negative self-talk involves cognitive distortions, such as overgeneralization or catastrophizing. Challenge these distortions by examining the evidence and considering alternative perspectives.

Self-Compassion: Practice self-compassion by treating yourself with the same kindness and understanding you would offer to a friend. Acknowledge your imperfections without judgment.

Cultivate Self-Encouragement: Replace self-criticism with self-encouragement. Focus on positive aspects of your experiences and remind yourself of your strengths and past successes.

Mindful Awareness: Practice mindfulness to observe negative thoughts without getting entangled in them. Mindfulness allows you to create distance from these thoughts and respond more skillfully.

Benefits of Overcoming Self-Criticism and Negative Self-Talk:

Improved Self-Esteem: Overcoming self-criticism promotes a healthier self-esteem by nurturing a more positive self-image.

Reduced Stress: Changing negative self-talk reduces stress by minimizing the impact of self-inflicted pressure and expectations.

Increased Resilience: Shifting towards self-compassion and positive self-talk enhances emotional resilience, helping you bounce back from challenges more effectively.

Better Mental Health: Overcoming self-criticism contributes to better mental well-being by reducing symptoms of anxiety and depression.

Healthy Relationships: Positive self-talk improves your self-image, leading to healthier relationships built on self-respect and authenticity.

Practical Steps to Overcome Self-Criticism and Negative Self-Talk:

Challenge Negative Statements: When negative thoughts arise, ask yourself if they are based on facts or assumptions. Challenge them with evidence to create a more balanced perspective.

Use Affirmations: Create positive affirmations that counteract negative beliefs. Repeat them regularly to reinforce a positive self-image.

Practice Gratitude: Focus on the positive aspects of your life and accomplishments. Regularly practice gratitude to shift your focus away from self-criticism.

Mindfulness Meditation: Engage in mindfulness meditation to observe your thoughts non-judgmentally and cultivate a sense of detachment from negative self-talk.

Seek Support: Reach out to friends, family, or a therapist for support and guidance in challenging and changing negative self-talk patterns.

In conclusion, overcoming self-criticism and negative self-talk is a transformative practice that enhances self-esteem, emotional well-being, and personal growth. By cultivating self-compassion, challenging distorted thoughts, and nurturing a positive internal dialogue, you can create a more nurturing and supportive relationship with yourself.

Cultivating self-compassion

Cultivating self-compassion is a vital component of the Practice of Self-Acceptance, which is one of the six pillars of self-esteem. Self-compassion involves treating yourself with kindness, understanding, and empathy, especially in times of difficulty or self-judgment. It is a practice that fosters a nurturing relationship with yourself and promotes a healthy sense of self-worth. Here's a detailed explanation of how to cultivate self-compassion:

Understanding Self-Compassion:

Self-compassion is the practice of extending the same warmth, care, and understanding to yourself that you would offer to a friend facing challenges. It involves recognizing your own humanity and embracing your imperfections with a gentle and supportive attitude.

Key Elements of Cultivating Self-Compassion:

Self-Kindness: Treat yourself with kindness and understanding, particularly when you're facing difficulties or making mistakes. Replace self-criticism with a compassionate inner dialogue.

Common Humanity: Acknowledge that everyone faces challenges and experiences moments of struggle. Recognize that you are not alone in your suffering, and that imperfection is a universal human experience.

Mindfulness: Practice mindfulness by observing your thoughts and feelings without judgment. This allows you to create space between your thoughts and your emotional reactions.

Self-Encouragement: Offer yourself words of encouragement and support. Acknowledge your efforts and progress, even when things don't go as planned.

Balance with Reality: While self-compassion is important, it doesn't mean ignoring mistakes or avoiding accountability. It's about addressing challenges with kindness while also taking responsibility for growth.

Benefits of Cultivating Self-Compassion:

Enhanced Self-Esteem: Cultivating self-compassion contributes to a healthier self-esteem by nurturing a positive self-image and reducing self-criticism.

Stress Reduction: Self-compassion reduces stress by providing a buffer against the negative impact of self-judgment and harsh self-talk.

Emotional Resilience: Practicing self-compassion enhances emotional resilience, allowing you to navigate challenges with greater ease and self-assurance.

Improved Mental Health: Self-compassion is associated with better mental well-being and reduced symptoms of anxiety and depression.

Healthy Relationships: Cultivating self-compassion improves your self-image, which positively impacts your relationships by fostering authenticity and self-respect.

Practical Steps to Cultivate Self-Compassion:

Self-Talk Awareness: Pay attention to your inner dialogue. When you notice self-criticism, replace it with kind and supportive words.

Self-Compassion Break: In challenging moments, take a self-compassion break. Acknowledge your pain, remind yourself that suffering is part of the human experience, and offer words of comfort.

Mindful Self-Compassion Meditation: Engage in guided mindfulness meditation practices that focus on self-compassion and nurturing self-kindness.

Write a Self-Compassionate Letter: Write a letter to yourself as if you were offering support and encouragement to a friend in a similar situation.

Practice Forgiveness: Forgive yourself for past mistakes and acknowledge that growth involves learning from experiences.

In conclusion, cultivating self-compassion is a transformative practice that enhances your relationship with yourself and contributes to a more positive self-esteem. By treating yourself with kindness, understanding, and empathy, you create a foundation of self-love that supports your well-being and personal growth.

Pillar 3: *The Practice of Self-Responsibility*

The Practice of Self-Responsibility is a significant pillar of self-esteem that involves taking ownership of your thoughts, feelings, actions, and life choices. It is the practice of recognizing that you are in control of your own life and outcomes, and that your decisions shape your reality. This pillar encourages empowerment, accountability, and a proactive approach to personal development. Let's delve into a detailed explanation of the third pillar:

Understanding Self-Responsibility:

Self-responsibility involves acknowledging your role as the primary agent in your life's journey. It is the practice of taking control of your decisions, behaviors, and responses to circumstances. Rather than blaming external factors, self-responsibility empowers you to make conscious choices that align with your values and goals.

Key Elements of Self-Responsibility:

Awareness: Self-responsibility begins with self-awareness – understanding your thoughts, emotions, and motivations. It's about recognizing the choices you have and their potential consequences.

Ownership: Taking ownership means acknowledging that your decisions and actions are your own. It involves accepting both the successes and challenges that arise from your choices.

Proactive Mindset: Self-responsibility promotes a proactive approach to life. Instead of reacting to circumstances, you take deliberate actions that lead to desired outcomes.

Problem-Solving: Embracing self-responsibility encourages you to seek solutions and take action when faced with challenges, rather than dwelling on problems.

Self-Determination: This practice emphasizes your autonomy and ability to create your own path. It reinforces that you have the power to shape your life's direction.

Benefits of Self-Responsibility:

Empowerment: Self-responsibility empowers you to make intentional decisions that lead to personal growth, achievement, and well-being.

Enhanced Self-Esteem: Taking ownership of your choices and actions boosts your self-esteem, as you see yourself as an active participant in your life.

Positive Decision-Making: Self-responsibility promotes thoughtful decision-making, considering long-term consequences and aligning choices with your values.

Resilience: Embracing self-responsibility builds resilience, as you view challenges as opportunities for growth and take actions to overcome them.

Healthy Relationships: When you take responsibility for your thoughts and behaviors, you contribute to healthier interactions and relationships.

Personal Growth: Self-responsibility fuels personal development by encouraging continuous learning, self-improvement, and adaptability.

Practical Steps to Practice Self-Responsibility:

Reflection: Regularly reflect on your choices, actions, and their outcomes. Consider how your decisions contribute to your current reality.

Accountability: Hold yourself accountable for your commitments and obligations. If you make a mistake, acknowledge it and take steps to rectify the situation.

Set Clear Goals: Define your goals and aspirations, then create actionable steps to achieve them. Take responsibility for making progress.

Embrace Challenges: View challenges as opportunities to demonstrate self-responsibility. Identify strategies to overcome obstacles and take action.

Learn from Mistakes: Instead of dwelling on failures, focus on the lessons learned and how you can use them to make better choices in the future.

In conclusion, the Practice of Self-Responsibility empowers you to take control of your life, make conscious choices, and actively shape your reality. By embracing self-awareness, ownership, and a proactive mindset, you build a foundation of self-esteem rooted in accountability and personal growth.

Taking ownership of one's actions and emotions

Taking ownership of one's actions and emotions is a crucial aspect of the Practice of Self-Responsibility, one of the six pillars of self-esteem. It involves recognizing that you have control over your behaviors, decisions, and emotional responses, and taking accountability for them. This practice empowers you to lead a more intentional and empowered life. Here's a detailed explanation of taking ownership of one's actions and emotions:

Understanding Ownership of Actions and Emotions:

Taking ownership means acknowledging that you are the source of your actions and emotions. It involves recognizing that you have the power to choose your responses and that your behaviors impact your life and the lives of others.

Key Elements of Taking Ownership:

Personal Responsibility: Taking ownership is about being accountable for your choices and actions, whether they lead to success or setbacks.

Awareness: Being aware of your actions and emotions is the first step in taking ownership. This requires self-reflection and self-awareness.

Choice: Recognize that you have the power to choose how you respond to situations and how you express your emotions.

Self-Regulation: Taking ownership involves managing your emotions and responses in a constructive and balanced manner.

Benefits of Taking Ownership:

Empowerment: Taking ownership empowers you to create positive change in your life. When you recognize your agency, you can make deliberate choices that align with your goals.

Improved Relationships: Ownership of actions and emotions fosters healthier relationships by promoting clear communication and accountability.

Enhanced Self-Esteem: Being accountable for your choices and emotional responses builds self-esteem, as you see yourself as an active participant in your life.

Effective Problem-Solving: Taking ownership encourages problem-solving skills. When you acknowledge your role, you can find solutions and make improvements.

Emotional Intelligence: Recognizing and regulating your emotions leads to greater emotional intelligence and healthier emotional expression.

Personal Growth: Taking ownership is a catalyst for personal growth and self-improvement, as you learn from experiences and make intentional changes.

Practical Steps to Take Ownership:

Reflect: Regularly reflect on your actions, decisions, and emotional responses. Consider how they align with your values and goals.

Practice Self-Awareness: Pay attention to your emotions as they arise. Identify triggers and patterns in your emotional responses.

Pause and Choose: Before reacting emotionally, take a moment to pause. Choose a response that aligns with your values and desired outcomes.

Apologize and Make Amends: If you make a mistake, take responsibility, apologize, and take steps to make amends if necessary.

Use "I" Statements: Express your emotions using "I" statements to take ownership of your feelings and communicate effectively.

Learn from Feedback: Accept feedback from others without defensiveness. Use it as an opportunity for growth and self-improvement.

In conclusion, taking ownership of one's actions and emotions is a transformative practice that promotes self-responsibility, personal growth, and a healthier sense of self-esteem. By recognizing your agency and actively choosing your responses, you empower yourself to lead a more intentional and fulfilling life.

Avoiding victim mentality

Avoiding victim mentality is an essential aspect of the Practice of Self-Responsibility, one of the six pillars of self-esteem. Victim mentality refers to a mindset where an individual perceives themselves as helpless and powerless, attributing their challenges and difficulties solely to external factors. Overcoming victim mentality involves taking ownership of one's circumstances, emotions, and responses, and adopting a proactive and empowered mindset. Here's a detailed explanation of avoiding victim mentality:

Understanding Victim Mentality:
Victim mentality is characterized by a belief that external forces have complete control over one's life and outcomes. Individuals with this mindset often perceive themselves as powerless, blaming others or circumstances for their challenges without acknowledging their role in the situation.

Key Elements of Avoiding Victim Mentality:

Self-Awareness: Recognize when you are slipping into a victim mentality by being mindful of your thoughts, language, and emotional responses.

Ownership: Shift from attributing challenges solely to external factors to acknowledging your own choices, behaviors, and responses that contribute to your circumstances.

Mindset Shift: Adopt a proactive mindset that focuses on taking action, problem-solving, and seeking opportunities for growth, rather than dwelling on setbacks.

Empowerment: Recognize your ability to influence and shape your life, even in the face of challenges. Embrace a sense of agency and control.

Benefits of Avoiding Victim Mentality:

Personal Empowerment: Overcoming victim mentality empowers you to take control of your life and make intentional choices that lead to personal growth.

Enhanced Self-Esteem: Avoiding victim mentality boosts your self-esteem by fostering a sense of ownership and self-worth.

Resilience: Cultivating a proactive mindset enhances resilience, enabling you to bounce back from setbacks and face challenges with strength.

Positive Relationships: Avoiding victim mentality improves relationships by promoting effective communication, accountability, and mutual respect.

Emotional Well-Being: Letting go of victim mentality contributes to better emotional well-being, as you develop healthier coping mechanisms and emotional regulation skills.

Practical Steps to Avoid Victim Mentality:

Challenge Thought Patterns: Identify negative thought patterns that perpetuate victim mentality. Challenge and reframe these thoughts with a focus on personal responsibility and empowerment.

Take Action: Instead of dwelling on problems, take proactive steps to address challenges and seek solutions.

Practice Gratitude: Cultivate a sense of gratitude for the positive aspects of your life, shifting your focus away from a victim mindset.

Set Goals: Set clear goals and create actionable plans to achieve them, focusing on what you can control.

Focus on Solutions: When facing challenges, shift your focus from blaming external factors to identifying practical solutions.

Seek Support: Reach out to friends, family, or professionals for guidance and encouragement in overcoming victim mentality.

In conclusion, avoiding victim mentality is a transformative practice that empowers you to take control of your life, make proactive choices, and cultivate a strong sense of self-esteem. By recognizing your agency and embracing a mindset of ownership, you can overcome challenges, achieve personal growth, and lead a more empowered and fulfilling life.

Setting and pursuing personal goals

Setting and pursuing personal goals is a crucial aspect of the Practice of Self-Responsibility, one of the six pillars of self-esteem. This practice involves defining meaningful objectives, creating actionable plans, and taking deliberate steps to achieve them. It empowers individuals to actively shape their lives, enhance their sense of accomplishment, and contribute to their self-esteem. Here's a detailed explanation of setting and pursuing personal goals:

Understanding Personal Goals:
Personal goals are specific, achievable targets that you set for yourself to improve various areas of your life. They can be related to career, health, relationships, personal development, or any other aspect that holds significance to you. Setting personal goals gives you direction and purpose, while pursuing them involves consistent effort and commitment.

Key Elements of Setting and Pursuing Personal Goals:

Clarity: Clearly define your goals, ensuring they are specific, measurable, achievable, relevant, and time-bound (SMART).

Motivation: Connect your goals to your values and aspirations to maintain strong motivation throughout the pursuit.

Action Plan: Break down each goal into smaller, manageable steps. Create an actionable plan outlining the tasks needed to achieve your objectives.

Commitment: Set a strong intention to pursue your goals, demonstrating dedication and discipline in your efforts.

Adaptability: Be open to adjusting your goals and plans as circumstances change, allowing flexibility while staying focused on the overarching objective.

Benefits of Setting and Pursuing Personal Goals:

Direction and Focus: Personal goals provide a clear sense of direction, helping you prioritize tasks and make informed decisions aligned with your aspirations.

Sense of Accomplishment: Pursuing and achieving goals boosts self-esteem by generating a sense of accomplishment and validation of your capabilities.

Motivation and Drive: Goals serve as motivators, fueling your determination and drive to overcome challenges and obstacles.

Personal Growth: The pursuit of goals encourages learning, skill development, and self-improvement, contributing to personal growth and self-awareness.

Enhanced Resilience: Goal pursuit cultivates resilience, as setbacks become opportunities for learning and adapting rather than discouragement.

Self-Efficacy: Successfully achieving goals enhances your self-efficacy – your belief in your ability to achieve future goals.

Practical Steps to Set and Pursue Personal Goals:

Identify Priorities: Determine which areas of your life you want to focus on and set goals that align with your values.

Set SMART Goals: Create goals that are Specific, Measurable, Achievable, Relevant, and Time-Bound.

Break Down Goals: Divide each goal into smaller steps to make the journey more manageable and less overwhelming.

Create an Action Plan: Outline the tasks, resources, and timelines required to achieve each goal.

Stay Accountable: Share your goals with a trusted friend or use tools like journals or apps to track progress and hold yourself accountable.

Celebrate Milestones: Celebrate your achievements along the way to maintain motivation and acknowledge your progress.

Learn from Challenges: Embrace setbacks as learning opportunities. Analyze challenges, adjust strategies, and continue moving forward.

In conclusion, setting and pursuing personal goals is a transformative practice that empowers you to take charge of your life, enhance self-esteem, and foster personal growth. By aligning your actions with your aspirations, you create a sense of purpose, accomplishment, and a strong foundation for the Practice of Self-Responsibility.

Pillar 4: The Practice of Self-Assertiveness

The Practice of Self-Assertiveness is a significant pillar of self-esteem that involves expressing your thoughts, needs, and desires confidently and respectfully while considering the rights and feelings of others. It is about standing up for yourself, setting healthy boundaries, and advocating for your well-being without compromising your integrity. This practice empowers individuals to assert their authentic selves and contribute to healthy relationships and a strong self-esteem. Here's a detailed explanation of the fourth pillar:

Understanding Self-Assertiveness:
Self-assertiveness is the practice of confidently communicating your thoughts, feelings, and needs, while respecting the perspectives of others. It involves expressing yourself honestly, setting boundaries, and making choices that align with your values and desires.

Key Elements of Self-Assertiveness:

Confidence: Self-assertiveness requires self-confidence and belief in the validity of your thoughts and feelings.

Effective Communication: It involves clear and respectful communication that conveys your thoughts and needs without infringing on the rights of others.

Boundary Setting: Self-assertiveness includes setting and maintaining boundaries to protect your well-being and integrity.

Self-Respect: Self-assertiveness is rooted in self-respect and a willingness to advocate for your rights and dignity.

Mutual Understanding: Effective self-assertiveness seeks to create a mutual understanding between you and others, fostering open dialogue.

Benefits of Self-Assertiveness:

Enhanced Self-Esteem: Self-assertiveness boosts self-esteem by affirming your worth, autonomy, and ability to communicate effectively.

Healthy Relationships: Practicing self-assertiveness contributes to healthier relationships built on respect, open communication, and mutual understanding.

Empowerment: Self-assertiveness empowers you to take charge of your life, make informed choices, and pursue your goals with confidence.

Conflict Resolution: Confidently expressing your needs and perspectives aids in resolving conflicts and misunderstandings.

Stress Reduction: Self-assertiveness reduces stress by preventing resentment from unexpressed feelings and promoting authenticity.

Practical Steps to Practice Self-Assertiveness:

Know Your Rights: Understand your rights and needs, and recognize that advocating for yourself is healthy and important.

Use "I" Statements: Express your thoughts and feelings using "I" statements to avoid blaming or accusing others.

Practice Active Listening: When asserting yourself, listen attentively to the responses of others and seek mutual understanding.

Set Clear Boundaries: Clearly communicate your boundaries and enforce them when necessary, respecting both your needs and the needs of others.

Practice Empathy: While asserting yourself, empathize with the perspectives of others and aim for a balance between your needs and theirs.

Start Small: Begin with low-stakes situations and gradually work your way up to more challenging assertiveness scenarios.

Seek Support: If needed, seek guidance from therapists or communication workshops to improve your self-assertiveness skills.

In conclusion, the Practice of Self-Assertiveness is a transformative pillar that empowers individuals to express themselves confidently, set boundaries, and foster healthy relationships. By embracing self-respect and effective communication, you contribute to a strong sense of self-esteem, personal growth, and meaningful connections with others.

Expressing one's needs, wants, and opinions assertively

Expressing one's needs, wants, and opinions assertively is a key component of the Practice of Self-Assertiveness, one of the six pillars of self-esteem. Assertive communication involves confidently expressing yourself while respecting the rights and feelings of others. It allows you to communicate effectively, set boundaries, and advocate for your well-being without resorting to aggression or passivity. Here's a detailed explanation of how to express needs, wants, and opinions assertively:

Understanding Assertive Expression:

Assertive expression is the art of communicating your thoughts, feelings, desires, and opinions in a clear, confident, and respectful manner. It involves advocating for yourself while considering the perspectives and rights of others. Assertive communication fosters open dialogue, builds healthy relationships, and enhances your self-esteem.

Key Elements of Assertive Expression:

Clarity: Clearly state your needs, wants, and opinions, using concise and direct language. Avoid ambiguity or vagueness.

Confidence: Express yourself with self-assurance and conviction, showing that you value your thoughts and feelings.

Respect for Others: Consider the feelings and viewpoints of others, ensuring that your expression is respectful and does not infringe on their rights.

Active Listening: While expressing yourself, actively listen to the responses of others, demonstrating your willingness to engage in a meaningful conversation.

Use of "I" Statements: Frame your statements using "I" rather than "you" to avoid sounding accusatory and to take ownership of your feelings and opinions.

Benefits of Assertive Expression:

Healthy Relationships: Assertive communication fosters healthy relationships by promoting open dialogue, mutual understanding, and respect.

Enhanced Self-Esteem: Expressing yourself assertively affirms your self-worth, contributing to higher self-esteem and self-confidence.

Conflict Resolution: Assertive expression helps resolve conflicts constructively by addressing issues directly and fostering cooperation.

Effective Problem-Solving: By clearly stating your needs and opinions, you facilitate effective problem-solving and decision-making.

Boundary Setting: Assertive communication allows you to establish and maintain healthy boundaries, protecting your well-being.

Practical Steps for Assertive Expression:

Prepare: Before communicating, organize your thoughts and clarify what you want to express.

Use "I" Statements: Begin your statements with "I feel," "I want," or "I believe," which conveys your perspective without placing blame.

Practice Active Listening: Give others your full attention and listen actively when they respond, showing your willingness to engage.

Choose the Right Time and Place: Find an appropriate setting for the conversation, ensuring minimal distractions and enough time for discussion.

Stay Calm: Maintain a composed demeanor, even if the conversation becomes emotional. Focus on the issue at hand.

Be Open to Compromise: While asserting your needs, be open to finding solutions that address the concerns of both parties.

Practice: Start with less challenging situations and gradually work your way up to more complex discussions.

In conclusion, expressing one's needs, wants, and opinions assertively is a transformative practice that enhances communication, relationships, and self-esteem. By confidently and respectfully advocating for yourself, you contribute to a stronger sense of self, improved interactions, and a deeper understanding of your own needs and values.

Resisting social pressures or manipulation

Resisting social pressures or manipulation is a vital aspect of the Practice of Self-Assertiveness, one of the six pillars of self-esteem. It involves staying true to your values, making independent decisions, and safeguarding your well-being against external influences that may attempt to sway or manipulate you. This practice empowers individuals to maintain their authenticity, autonomy, and self-respect. Here's a detailed explanation of how to resist social pressures or manipulation:

Understanding Resisting Social Pressures or Manipulation: Resisting social pressures or manipulation involves recognizing and challenging external influences that seek to control or alter your thoughts, behaviors, or decisions. It requires asserting your autonomy and making choices that align with your values, even when faced with societal expectations or manipulation tactics.

Key Elements of Resisting Social Pressures or Manipulation:

Self-Awareness: Be aware of your own values, beliefs, and priorities, which serve as your foundation for resisting external pressures.

Critical Thinking: Engage in critical thinking to evaluate messages, opinions, and requests that may be aimed at manipulating or pressuring you.

Assertiveness: Confidently express your decisions and boundaries, even in the face of external pressure or manipulation attempts.

Independence: Make decisions based on your authentic self rather than conforming to others' expectations or manipulation tactics.

Emotional Regulation: Develop emotional resilience to handle any discomfort or guilt that may arise when resisting social pressures.

Benefits of Resisting Social Pressures or Manipulation:

Authenticity: Resisting external pressures fosters authenticity, allowing you to make choices that align with your true self.

Enhanced Self-Esteem: Standing up against manipulation or social pressures reinforces your self-worth and boosts self-esteem.

Empowerment: The practice empowers you to take control of your life, decisions, and well-being.

Healthy Boundaries: Resisting manipulation contributes to establishing and maintaining healthy boundaries in relationships.

Personal Growth: By making independent choices, you promote personal growth and self-awareness.

Practical Steps to Resist Social Pressures or Manipulation:

Clarify Values: Reflect on your values and priorities, which serve as a compass for making independent decisions.

Question Messages: Critically assess messages, requests, or opinions before accepting or acting upon them.

Use Delayed Response: When faced with pressure or manipulation, take time to respond rather than giving an immediate answer.

Practice Saying No: Learn to say "no" assertively and respectfully when a situation or request does not align with your values or goals.

Seek Support: Confide in trusted friends or mentors who can provide guidance and support in resisting manipulation or social pressures.

Set Personal Boundaries: Clearly define your boundaries and communicate them to others, reinforcing your commitment to your well-being.

Educate Yourself: Learn about manipulation tactics, cognitive biases, and persuasive techniques to be more resistant to them.

In conclusion, resisting social pressures or manipulation is a transformative practice that empowers you to make independent decisions, stay true to your values, and protect your well-being. By asserting your autonomy and maintaining authenticity, you contribute to a stronger sense of self-esteem, personal growth, and meaningful relationships based on mutual respect.

Honoring one's values and boundaries

Honoring one's values and boundaries is a crucial aspect of the Practice of Self-Assertiveness, one of the six pillars of self-esteem. This practice involves recognizing and respecting your core values, setting clear boundaries to protect your well-being, and aligning your choices and actions with what is truly important to you. Honoring your values and boundaries empowers you to live authentically, make meaningful decisions, and cultivate self-respect. Here's a detailed explanation:

Understanding Honoring Values and Boundaries:
Honoring values and boundaries involves acknowledging the principles that guide your life and ensuring that your actions and decisions align with those principles. It also includes setting and communicating personal boundaries to maintain your emotional, physical, and psychological well-being.

Key Elements of Honoring Values and Boundaries:

Self-Reflection: Take time to reflect on your values – the beliefs and principles that hold significance in your life.

Boundary Setting: Define and communicate clear boundaries that protect your physical, emotional, and mental space.

Consistency: Strive for consistency between your actions and your values, even when faced with challenges or external pressures.

Assertive Communication: Clearly and confidently express your boundaries and values to others, ensuring mutual understanding.

Self-Respect: Honoring your values and boundaries demonstrates self-respect and self-care, showing that you prioritize your well-being.

Benefits of Honoring Values and Boundaries:

Authentic Living: Aligning your choices with your values leads to authentic living, fostering a sense of purpose and fulfillment.

Enhanced Self-Esteem: Honoring your values and boundaries reinforces your self-worth, boosting self-esteem and self-confidence.

Healthy Relationships: Clearly communicated boundaries contribute to healthier relationships built on mutual respect and understanding.

Emotional Well-Being: Respecting your boundaries protects your emotional well-being and prevents emotional exhaustion.

Reduced Stress: Making decisions in line with your values and maintaining boundaries reduces internal conflict and stress.

Practical Steps to Honor Values and Boundaries:

Identify Core Values: Reflect on the values that matter most to you, such as honesty, integrity, compassion, or personal growth.

Set Clear Boundaries: Define boundaries for different aspects of your life, such as relationships, work, and personal time.

Communicate Boundaries: Clearly and respectfully communicate your boundaries to others, explaining why they are important to you.

Practice Saying No: Learn to say "no" assertively when a situation or request does not align with your values or boundaries.

Regular Self-Check: Periodically assess your actions and decisions to ensure they are consistent with your values and boundaries.

Seek Support: If needed, seek guidance from trusted friends, family members, or professionals in maintaining and communicating boundaries.

Self-Compassion: Be kind to yourself if you encounter challenges in upholding your boundaries. Remember that honoring your values is a process.

In conclusion, honoring one's values and boundaries is a transformative practice that empowers you to live authentically, protect your well-being, and cultivate self-respect. By aligning your actions with your values and communicating clear boundaries, you contribute to a strong sense of self-esteem, meaningful relationships, and a more fulfilled life.

Pillar 5: The Practice of Living Purposefully

The Practice of Living Purposefully is a significant pillar of self-esteem that involves identifying and pursuing meaningful goals, activities, and passions that align with your values and bring a sense of fulfillment and purpose to your life. This practice encourages individuals to lead intentional, goal-oriented lives that contribute to personal growth, self-worth, and a deeper sense of meaning. Here's a detailed explanation of the fifth pillar:

Understanding Living Purposefully:
Living purposefully involves actively seeking out and engaging in activities that resonate with your values, interests, and aspirations. It means living with intention, setting meaningful goals, and making choices that contribute to your overall well-being and sense of purpose.

Key Elements of Living Purposefully:

Clarity: Gain clarity about your values, passions, and long-term aspirations to guide your decisions and actions.

Goal-Setting: Set specific, measurable, achievable, relevant, and time-bound (SMART) goals that align with your values and purpose.

Focus: Prioritize activities and pursuits that contribute to your goals and align with your purpose, minimizing distractions.

Engagement: Fully engage in your chosen activities, investing your time, energy, and enthusiasm to create meaningful experiences.

Mindful Presence: Practice mindfulness and be fully present in each moment, embracing the journey toward your goals.

Benefits of Living Purposefully:

Enhanced Self-Esteem: Living purposefully reinforces your sense of self-worth by actively pursuing activities that align with your values and goals.

Fulfillment: Engaging in purposeful activities brings a sense of fulfillment and joy, contributing to overall well-being.

Motivation: Having a clear sense of purpose fuels intrinsic motivation, propelling you to work toward your goals with determination.

Resilience: Living purposefully enhances resilience, as your sense of purpose provides a source of strength during challenges.

Personal Growth: Pursuing meaningful goals and activities encourages continuous learning and personal development.

Practical Steps to Practice Living Purposefully:

Reflect: Reflect on your values, passions, and aspirations to gain clarity about what brings you meaning and fulfillment.

Set Goals: Define both short-term and long-term goals that align with your purpose and values.

Prioritize: Prioritize activities that contribute to your goals and purpose, allocating your time and resources accordingly.

Minimize Distractions: Identify and reduce activities or habits that detract from your purposeful pursuits.

Embrace Learning: Embrace challenges and setbacks as opportunities for learning and growth on your purposeful journey.

Stay Present: Practice mindfulness to stay present and fully engaged in each moment, fostering a deeper connection to your purpose.

Regular Review: Periodically review your goals and activities to ensure they continue to align with your evolving sense of purpose.

In conclusion, the Practice of Living Purposefully is a transformative pillar that empowers you to lead a life of intention, meaning, and self-worth. By identifying and pursuing activities that align with your values and goals, you contribute to a stronger sense of self-esteem, personal growth, and a more fulfilling and purposeful life.

Identifying and pursuing meaningful goals

Identifying and pursuing meaningful goals is a central aspect of the Practice of Living Purposefully, one of the six pillars of self-esteem. This practice involves recognizing what truly matters to you, setting goals that align with your values and aspirations, and taking intentional actions to achieve them. By identifying and pursuing meaningful goals, you cultivate a sense of purpose, personal fulfillment, and a stronger sense of self-esteem. Here's a detailed explanation of how to identify and pursue meaningful goals:

Understanding Identifying and Pursuing Meaningful Goals: Identifying and pursuing meaningful goals means selecting objectives that resonate with your core values, passions, and vision for your life. These goals hold personal significance and contribute to your overall sense of purpose, guiding your actions and decisions.

Key Elements of Identifying and Pursuing Meaningful Goals:

Self-Reflection: Reflect on your values, interests, strengths, and aspirations to gain insight into what truly matters to you.

Clarity: Clearly define your goals, making them specific, measurable, achievable, relevant, and time-bound (SMART).

Alignment: Ensure your goals align with your values and overarching life purpose, creating a sense of cohesion and fulfillment.

Commitment: Make a dedicated commitment to your goals, demonstrating your willingness to invest time, effort, and resources.

Action Plan: Create a detailed plan outlining the steps and strategies required to achieve your meaningful goals.

Benefits of Identifying and Pursuing Meaningful Goals:

Enhanced Self-Esteem: Pursuing meaningful goals reinforces your sense of self-worth and accomplishment, boosting self-esteem.

Sense of Purpose: Identifying and pursuing meaningful goals provides a clear sense of purpose, guiding your daily actions and decisions.

Motivation: Meaningful goals fuel intrinsic motivation, driving you to overcome challenges and stay committed.

Personal Growth: Pursuing meaningful goals encourages continuous learning, skill development, and personal growth.

Fulfillment: Achieving meaningful goals brings a deep sense of satisfaction and fulfillment, contributing to overall well-being.

Practical Steps to Identify and Pursue Meaningful Goals:

Self-Reflection: Take time to introspect and identify your core values, passions, and aspirations.

Set Clear Goals: Define your goals using the SMART criteria to ensure they are specific and attainable.

Prioritize: Select a few key goals that have the most significant impact on your life and align with your purpose.

Break Down Goals: Divide each goal into smaller, manageable tasks to make the journey less overwhelming.

Create an Action Plan: Develop a detailed plan that outlines the steps, resources, and timelines needed to achieve each goal.

Stay Flexible: Be open to adjusting your goals and strategies as circumstances evolve.

Track Progress: Regularly monitor your progress and celebrate milestones, reinforcing your commitment and motivation.

Seek Support: Seek guidance from mentors, coaches, or supportive peers who can provide insights and encouragement.

In conclusion, identifying and pursuing meaningful goals is a transformative practice that empowers you to live with intention, purpose, and self-esteem. By aligning your actions with your values and aspirations, you contribute to personal growth, fulfillment, and a deeper sense of meaning in your life.

Aligning actions with personal values

Aligning actions with personal values is a fundamental component of the Practice of Living Purposefully, one of the six pillars of self-esteem. This practice involves consciously making choices and decisions that reflect your core beliefs, principles, and priorities. By ensuring that your actions are in harmony with your values, you create a life that is meaningful, authentic, and fulfilling. Here's a detailed explanation of how to align actions with personal values:

Understanding Aligning Actions with Personal Values:
Aligning actions with personal values means consistently making choices and taking actions that are in accordance with your deeply held beliefs, ethics, and aspirations. It involves living authentically and intentionally, ensuring that your behaviors are a reflection of what matters most to you.

Key Elements of Aligning Actions with Personal Values:

Self-Reflection: Engage in self-reflection to identify your core values and understand why they are important to you.

Awareness: Be mindful of your actions and decisions, considering whether they align with your values before taking any course of action.

Intentionality: Make conscious choices that reflect your values, even when faced with challenges or external pressures.

Consistency: Strive for consistency by aligning your actions with your values across various areas of your life.

Adaptability: While maintaining alignment, be open to adapting your actions to changing circumstances or new insights.

Benefits of Aligning Actions with Personal Values:

Authenticity: Aligning actions with personal values promotes authenticity and enables you to live in accordance with your true self.

Enhanced Self-Esteem: Consistently living by your values reinforces your self-worth and boosts self-esteem.

Sense of Purpose: Living in alignment with your values provides a sense of purpose and direction in your life.

Inner Harmony: When actions match values, you experience greater inner harmony, reduced cognitive dissonance, and increased emotional well-being.

Meaningful Living: Aligning actions with personal values leads to a more meaningful and fulfilling life.

Practical Steps to Align Actions with Personal Values:

Identify Core Values: Reflect on your beliefs and priorities to identify your core values, such as honesty, compassion, integrity, or family.

Evaluate Choices: Before making decisions, consider whether the options align with your values and prioritize those that do.

Practice Mindfulness: Be present and mindful as you make choices, ensuring they are in line with your values.

Set Priorities: Determine the relative importance of your values to guide decision-making when values may conflict.

Seek Guidance: When faced with difficult decisions, seek advice from mentors, friends, or professionals who share your values.

Review and Adjust: Regularly assess your actions to ensure they remain consistent with your values and make adjustments as needed.

Celebrate Alignment: Acknowledge and celebrate moments when your actions align with your values, reinforcing positive behaviors.

In conclusion, aligning actions with personal values is a transformative practice that empowers you to live a life of authenticity, purpose, and self-esteem. By consciously making choices that reflect your core beliefs, you create a meaningful and fulfilling journey that contributes to your overall well-being and sense of self.

Fostering a sense of purpose and fulfillment

Fostering a sense of purpose and fulfillment is a core objective of the Practice of Living Purposefully, one of the six pillars of self-esteem. This practice involves actively seeking and cultivating activities, goals, and experiences that bring a deep sense of meaning and satisfaction to your life. By nurturing a sense of purpose and fulfillment, you enhance your self-esteem, overall well-being, and create a foundation for a meaningful life. Here's a detailed explanation of how to foster a sense of purpose and fulfillment:

Understanding Fostering a Sense of Purpose and Fulfillment: Fostering a sense of purpose and fulfillment means engaging in activities and pursuits that align with your values, passions, and aspirations, leading to a profound and lasting sense of satisfaction. It involves seeking experiences that resonate with your innermost desires and contribute to a meaningful life.

Key Elements of Fostering a Sense of Purpose and Fulfillment:

Self-Discovery: Engage in self-discovery to identify your passions, strengths, values, and long-term aspirations.

Goal-Setting: Set both short-term and long-term goals that align with your values and contribute to your sense of purpose.

Engagement: Fully immerse yourself in activities that resonate with you, investing time, energy, and enthusiasm.

Meaningful Relationships: Cultivate connections with people who share your values and support your journey toward purpose and fulfillment.

Gratitude: Practice gratitude by appreciating and acknowledging the positive aspects of your life, fostering a sense of contentment.

Benefits of Fostering a Sense of Purpose and Fulfillment:

Enhanced Self-Esteem: Engaging in purposeful activities and pursuing fulfillment reinforces your self-worth and self-esteem.

Joy and Satisfaction: Fostering a sense of purpose brings joy and deep satisfaction, contributing to overall well-being.

Resilience: A strong sense of purpose enhances resilience, helping you navigate challenges with determination and optimism.

Improved Mental Health: Engaging in meaningful pursuits has been linked to reduced stress, anxiety, and depression.

Increased Motivation: A sense of purpose fuels intrinsic motivation, providing the drive to overcome obstacles and pursue your goals.

Practical Steps to Foster a Sense of Purpose and Fulfillment:

Self-Reflect: Reflect on your passions, values, strengths, and aspirations to gain insight into what brings you meaning.

Set Meaningful Goals: Set goals that align with your values and contribute to a sense of purpose in various aspects of your life.

Engage Fully: Immerse yourself in activities you enjoy and find meaningful, dedicating your time and energy to them.

Contribute to Others: Engage in acts of kindness, volunteering, or helping others, which can contribute to a sense of purpose.

Cultivate Gratitude: Regularly practice gratitude by acknowledging the positive aspects of your life and experiences.

Embrace Challenges: Embrace challenges and setbacks as opportunities for growth and learning on your journey toward fulfillment.

Seek Professional Help: If you're struggling to find a sense of purpose, consider seeking guidance from therapists or life coaches.

In conclusion, fostering a sense of purpose and fulfillment is a transformative practice that enhances your self-esteem, well-being, and overall quality of life. By engaging in activities that resonate with your values and aspirations, you create a life rich in meaning, satisfaction, and a deeper connection to yourself and the world around you.

Pillar 6: The Practice of Personal Integrity

The Practice of Personal Integrity is a foundational pillar of self-esteem that revolves around living in alignment with your values, principles, and ethical standards. It involves consistently acting in a way that reflects your authenticity, honesty, and moral convictions, regardless of external influences or pressures. This practice empowers individuals to cultivate a strong sense of self-worth, build trust with others, and lead a life characterized by ethical behavior and self-respect. Here's a detailed explanation of the sixth pillar:

Understanding Personal Integrity:
Personal integrity is the practice of upholding your values, ethics, and moral principles in your thoughts, actions, and interactions. It involves living authentically, making decisions that align with your inner compass, and demonstrating consistency between your beliefs and behaviors.

Key Elements of Personal Integrity:

Self-Awareness: Develop a deep understanding of your core values, beliefs, and ethical standards.

Consistency: Ensure that your actions are in harmony with your values, regardless of external circumstances.

Authenticity: Be true to yourself, avoiding hypocrisy or acting in ways that contradict your genuine beliefs.

Honesty: Practice honesty and transparency in your interactions, refraining from deception or manipulation.

Accountability: Take responsibility for your actions, acknowledging mistakes and making amends when necessary.

Benefits of Practicing Personal Integrity:

Enhanced Self-Esteem: Living with personal integrity reinforces your self-worth and self-respect, boosting self-esteem.

Trustworthiness: Demonstrating integrity builds trust with others, fostering healthy relationships and connections.

Inner Harmony: Aligning your actions with your values leads to a sense of inner harmony and reduced cognitive dissonance.

Ethical Leadership: Personal integrity sets a positive example, inspiring others to uphold their values and ethical standards.

Respected Reputation: Consistent ethical behavior contributes to a respected and positive reputation in both personal and professional spheres.

Practical Steps to Practice Personal Integrity:

Define Your Values: Reflect on your beliefs and values, clarifying the principles that guide your decisions.

Commit to Honesty: Prioritize honesty and authenticity in all your interactions, even when faced with difficult situations.

Reflect on Decisions: Before making decisions, consider whether they align with your values and ethical standards.

Accountability and Apology: Acknowledge and take responsibility for any actions that deviate from your values, and offer genuine apologies when needed.

Set Boundaries: Establish clear personal boundaries that reflect your values and communicate them effectively to others.

Be Consistent: Strive for consistency in your behavior, ensuring that your actions align with your beliefs over time.

Seek Feedback: Invite feedback from trusted friends or mentors to help you stay accountable to your principles.

In conclusion, the Practice of Personal Integrity is a transformative pillar that empowers you to live authentically, uphold ethical standards, and cultivate a strong sense of self-esteem and self-respect. By aligning your actions with your values and demonstrating integrity in your interactions, you contribute to a life marked by ethical behavior, trustworthiness, and meaningful relationships.

Maintaining congruence between actions and values

Maintaining congruence between actions and values is a vital aspect of the Practice of Personal Integrity, one of the six pillars of self-esteem. This practice involves ensuring that your behaviors, decisions, and choices align consistently with your core beliefs, principles, and ethical standards. By living in congruence with your values, you cultivate authenticity, self-respect, and a strong sense of self-esteem. Here's a detailed explanation of how to maintain congruence between actions and values:

Understanding Maintaining Congruence between Actions and Values:

Maintaining congruence means ensuring that there is harmony and consistency between what you believe and how you behave. It involves living in a way that reflects your true self, both in private and public settings, and making choices that are aligned with your deeply held values.

Key Elements of Maintaining Congruence between Actions and Values:

Self-Awareness: Develop a clear understanding of your values, beliefs, and ethical standards.

Alignment: Strive to align your decisions and behaviors with your values, avoiding contradictions or hypocrisy.

Integrity: Uphold your principles even when faced with challenges, pressures, or temptations.

Transparency: Be transparent and honest about your actions, avoiding deception or misrepresentation.

Accountability: Take responsibility for any discrepancies between your actions and values, and take steps to correct them.

Benefits of Maintaining Congruence between Actions and Values:

Enhanced Self-Esteem: Living in congruence with your values reinforces your self-worth and boosts self-esteem.

Authenticity: Maintaining congruence allows you to live authentically, being true to yourself in all situations.

Trustworthiness: Demonstrating consistency between your values and actions builds trust with others.

Inner Harmony: Congruence brings a sense of inner peace and reduces cognitive dissonance.

Ethical Leadership: Leading by example with congruence inspires others to uphold their values and principles.

Practical Steps to Maintain Congruence between Actions and Values:

Clarify Your Values: Reflect on your beliefs and identify the core values that guide your life.

Evaluate Decisions: Before making decisions, consider whether they align with your values and ethical standards.

Reflect on Actions: Regularly assess your actions and behaviors to ensure they remain consistent with your values.

Seek Guidance: When faced with challenging decisions, seek advice from mentors or trusted friends who share your values.

Take Responsibility: If you notice any discrepancies, take responsibility for your actions and make amends if necessary.

Practice Mindfulness: Be mindful of your choices and actions, consciously ensuring they align with your values.

Stay Resilient: Uphold your values even in challenging situations, demonstrating your commitment to personal integrity.

In conclusion, maintaining congruence between actions and values is a transformative practice that empowers you to live authentically, uphold ethical standards, and foster a strong sense of self-esteem and self-respect. By consistently aligning your behaviors with your values, you contribute to a life characterized by integrity, trustworthiness, and meaningful relationships.

Being honest and authentic in interactions

Being honest and authentic in interactions is a crucial component of the Practice of Personal Integrity, one of the six pillars of self-esteem. This practice involves communicating openly and genuinely, presenting yourself as you truly are, and conducting yourself with transparency and truthfulness. By embracing honesty and authenticity, you foster trust, strengthen relationships, and cultivate a sense of self-esteem based on integrity and genuine self-expression. Here's a detailed explanation of how to be honest and authentic in interactions:

Understanding Being Honest and Authentic in Interactions:
Being honest and authentic means expressing your thoughts, feelings, and intentions truthfully and openly, without pretense or deception. It involves showing your true self to others, building connections based on trust and transparency.

Key Elements of Being Honest and Authentic:

Self-Awareness: Develop a clear understanding of your thoughts, feelings, values, and intentions.

Transparency: Communicate openly and truthfully, avoiding hidden agendas or manipulation.

Genuine Expression: Express your true thoughts and emotions, avoiding pretending to be someone you're not.

Consistency: Maintain consistency between your words and actions, ensuring your behavior aligns with your intentions.

Respectful Communication: Be honest while considering the feelings and perspectives of others, using empathy and tact.

Benefits of Being Honest and Authentic in Interactions:

Enhanced Self-Esteem: Being honest and authentic reinforces your self-worth and self-respect, boosting self-esteem.

Trust: Demonstrating honesty and authenticity fosters trust in your relationships and interactions.

Stronger Connections: Authenticity forms deeper and more meaningful connections with others.

Emotional Well-Being: Expressing your true self reduces inner conflict and contributes to emotional well-being.

Respected Reputation: Consistently honest and authentic behavior leads to a respected and positive reputation.

Practical Steps to Be Honest and Authentic in Interactions:

Self-Reflection: Reflect on your thoughts, feelings, and values to gain self-awareness before interactions.

Open Communication: Communicate openly and transparently, sharing your thoughts and feelings truthfully.

Avoid Pretense: Be yourself, avoiding pretense or presenting a false image to gain approval.

Listen Actively: Listen attentively to others, demonstrating respect and empathy for their perspectives.

Own Your Mistakes: Acknowledge and take responsibility for any mistakes or errors, showing accountability.

Use "I" Statements: Express your feelings and opinions using "I" statements, which show ownership of your thoughts.

Practice Empathy: Put yourself in others' shoes, considering how your words and actions may affect them.

Stay Committed: Uphold honesty and authenticity consistently, even when faced with challenging situations.

In conclusion, being honest and authentic in interactions is a transformative practice that empowers you to build trust, strengthen relationships, and cultivate a strong sense of self-esteem. By communicating openly, transparently, and genuinely, you contribute to a life characterized by integrity, meaningful connections, and a deep sense of self-respect.

Building trust and credibility

Building trust and credibility is a fundamental aspect of the Practice of Personal Integrity, one of the six pillars of self-esteem. This practice involves demonstrating consistent honesty, reliability, and transparency in your actions and interactions with others. By establishing trust and credibility, you cultivate meaningful relationships, enhance your self-esteem, and contribute to a positive reputation. Here's a detailed explanation of how to build trust and credibility:

Understanding Building Trust and Credibility:
Building trust and credibility means consistently demonstrating integrity, reliability, and transparency in your interactions. It involves earning the confidence and respect of others through your actions, words, and behaviors.

Key Elements of Building Trust and Credibility:

Consistent Behavior: Act consistently and predictably, maintaining alignment between your words and actions.

Honesty: Communicate truthfully and openly, even when sharing challenging or difficult information.

Reliability: Fulfill your commitments and promises, showing that others can count on you.

Transparency: Share relevant information and intentions openly, avoiding hidden agendas or deceit.

Accountability: Take responsibility for your actions, admit mistakes, and work to make amends if necessary.

Benefits of Building Trust and Credibility:

Enhanced Self-Esteem: Building trust and credibility reinforces your self-worth and boosts self-esteem.

Stronger Relationships: Trust forms the foundation of strong, meaningful, and enduring relationships.

Effective Communication: Trust and credibility facilitate open and effective communication with others.

Positive Reputation: Demonstrating trustworthiness contributes to a positive reputation in personal and professional settings.

Collaboration: Trusted individuals are more likely to be sought after for collaboration and leadership roles.

Practical Steps to Build Trust and Credibility:

Be Consistent: Ensure that your actions align with your words consistently over time.

Fulfill Commitments: Honor your promises and commitments, even if they are small or seemingly insignificant.

Communicate Clearly: Be transparent and clear in your communication, avoiding ambiguity or hidden meanings.

Listen Actively: Show genuine interest in others' perspectives and concerns, actively listening and responding.

Own Mistakes: Admit mistakes and take responsibility for any errors, showing accountability and a willingness to learn.

Avoid Gossip: Refrain from engaging in negative or harmful gossip that could erode trust.

Prioritize Confidentiality: Respect others' confidentiality and privacy, demonstrating your trustworthiness.

Provide Feedback: Offer constructive feedback when appropriate, demonstrating your commitment to growth and improvement.

In conclusion, building trust and credibility is a transformative practice that empowers you to create strong relationships, enhance your self-esteem, and contribute to a positive and respected reputation. By consistently demonstrating honesty, reliability, and transparency, you foster an environment of trust, meaningful connections, and mutual respect.

CHAPTER 3

THE INTERPLAY OF THE SIX PILLARS

How the pillars reinforce each other

The six pillars of self-esteem are interconnected and reinforce each other in a powerful and synergistic way. Each pillar contributes to the development of a strong and healthy sense of self-esteem, and their combined practice leads to a more fulfilling and meaningful life. Here's a detailed explanation of how the pillars reinforce each other:

Living Consciously and Self-Awareness: The practice of living consciously, which involves self-awareness and mindfulness, lays the foundation for the other pillars. Being present in daily activities and accepting responsibility for your choices requires a heightened self-awareness. By understanding your thoughts, emotions, and behaviors, you can make more intentional decisions that align with your values and goals.

Self-Acceptance and Recognizing Strengths/Weaknesses: The practice of self-acceptance is closely intertwined with recognizing and embracing your strengths and weaknesses. When you accept yourself without judgment, you're more likely to acknowledge your strengths and utilize them while also addressing your weaknesses with self-compassion. This integration helps you develop a more balanced and authentic self-image.

Self-Responsibility and Personal Integrity: Taking ownership of your actions and emotions contributes to building personal integrity. When you practice self-responsibility, you demonstrate accountability for your choices, which is a key aspect of personal integrity. Your commitment to upholding your values and being honest and authentic in interactions further reinforces your sense of responsibility.

Living Purposefully and Fostering a Sense of Purpose/Fulfillment: The practice of living purposefully involves setting and pursuing meaningful goals that align with your values. By fostering a sense of purpose and fulfillment, you enhance your motivation and intrinsic drive to achieve those goals. The pursuit of meaningful goals also contributes to a deeper sense of self-worth and authenticity.

Personal Integrity and Being Honest/Authentic: Personal integrity, which emphasizes honesty and authenticity, is closely linked to the other pillars. Being honest and authentic in interactions is an essential aspect of personal integrity. When you act with integrity, you build trust and credibility, which, in turn, support your ability to maintain congruence between your actions and values.

Building Trust/Credibility and Self-Respect: Building trust and credibility involves demonstrating consistent honesty, reliability, and transparency. This practice contributes to a positive reputation and reinforces your self-respect. When you are trustworthy and credible, you strengthen your self-esteem by affirming your ability to uphold your values and make meaningful contributions to others.

The interconnectedness of the pillars creates a cycle of positive reinforcement. As you engage in each practice, you enhance various aspects of your self-esteem, leading to a more holistic and empowered sense of self. This integrated approach helps you navigate life with authenticity, purpose, and a strong foundation of self-worth.

Examples of how lacking in one pillar can impact others

Lacking proficiency in one pillar of self-esteem can have a cascading effect, negatively impacting other pillars and overall well-being. The interconnected nature of the pillars means that deficiencies in one area can create challenges and limitations in multiple aspects of your life. Here are examples of how lacking in one pillar can impact others:

Lacking in Self-Acceptance:

Impact on Personal Integrity: Without self-acceptance, you might be tempted to present a false image of yourself to gain approval or avoid judgment, compromising your personal integrity.

Impact on Living Purposefully: A lack of self-acceptance can lead to pursuing goals that don't align with your true self, resulting in a lack of fulfillment and purpose.

Lacking in Self-Responsibility:

Impact on Living Consciously: Avoiding responsibility for your choices can lead to mindless decision-making, disconnecting you from the practice of living consciously.

Impact on Building Trust/Credibility: Failure to take responsibility for your actions erodes trust and credibility, as others may perceive you as unreliable or unaccountable.

Lacking in Living Purposefully:

Impact on Self-Awareness: Neglecting to live purposefully can lead to a lack of self-awareness, as you may not take the time to reflect on your values and aspirations.

Impact on Fostering a Sense of Purpose/Fulfillment: Without purposeful living, you might struggle to set meaningful goals, hindering your ability to experience a sense of fulfillment.

Lacking in Personal Integrity:

Impact on Being Honest/Authentic: A lack of personal integrity can lead to dishonesty and inauthenticity in interactions, making it challenging to build trust and credibility.

Impact on Recognizing Strengths/Weaknesses: Lack of integrity might hinder your ability to acknowledge and address your weaknesses, preventing balanced self-awareness.

Lacking in Building Trust/Credibility:

Impact on Living Consciously: A lack of trustworthiness can lead to inner turmoil and cognitive dissonance, disrupting your ability to live consciously and mindfully.

Impact on Self-Respect: Failing to build trust and credibility can undermine your self-respect, as you may doubt your ability to uphold your values.

Lacking in Living Consciously:

Impact on Fostering a Sense of Purpose/Fulfillment: Ignoring the practice of living consciously may result in pursuing goals that lack alignment with your values, leading to a lack of fulfillment.

Impact on Expressing Needs/Wants/Opinions Assertively: A lack of mindfulness can hinder your ability to communicate assertively, as you may not fully understand your own needs and desires.

These examples illustrate the interconnectedness of the pillars and how deficiencies in one area can create challenges in others. Strengthening each pillar contributes to a more balanced and empowered sense of self, leading to enhanced overall well-being and a more meaningful and fulfilling life.

Cultivating a balanced and holistic self-esteem

Cultivating a balanced and holistic self-esteem involves nurturing all six pillars of self-esteem in a harmonious and integrated manner. This approach focuses on developing a comprehensive sense of self-worth that is grounded in self-awareness, authenticity, and a strong alignment with personal values. By nurturing each pillar, you create a well-rounded foundation for healthy self-esteem and a more fulfilling life. Here's a detailed explanation of how to cultivate a balanced and holistic self-esteem:

Understanding Cultivating a Balanced and Holistic Self-Esteem: Cultivating a balanced and holistic self-esteem means actively engaging with each of the six pillars—Living Consciously, Self-Acceptance, Self-Responsibility, Living Purposefully, Personal Integrity, and Building Trust/Credibility. By integrating these practices into your daily life, you create a comprehensive and interconnected sense of self-esteem.

Key Elements of Cultivating Balanced and Holistic Self-Esteem:

Integration: Integrate the practices of each pillar into your lifestyle, ensuring that they complement and support each other.

Awareness: Be conscious of your thoughts, behaviors, and decisions, consistently striving for self-awareness and mindfulness.

Consistency: Practice each pillar consistently over time, recognizing that ongoing effort is required to maintain balance.

Self-Reflection: Regularly reflect on your progress, identifying areas of strength and opportunities for growth.

Adaptability: Be open to adapting your practices based on changing circumstances and new insights.

Benefits of Cultivating Balanced and Holistic Self-Esteem:

Comprehensive Well-Being: Balancing the pillars enhances various aspects of your well-being, including emotional, social, and psychological dimensions.

Resilience: A holistic self-esteem equips you with the resilience to navigate challenges, setbacks, and uncertainties.

Authenticity: A balanced self-esteem enables you to live authentically and make decisions aligned with your true self.

Positive Relationships: Nurturing all pillars fosters trust, effective communication, and deeper connections in relationships.

Purposeful Living: Cultivating a holistic self-esteem guides you toward purposeful living, setting and pursuing meaningful goals.

Practical Steps to Cultivate Balanced and Holistic Self-Esteem:

Set Intentions: Set an intention to engage with each pillar, dedicating time and effort to develop a well-rounded self-esteem.

Prioritize Growth: Identify areas where you feel less proficient and prioritize their development.

Create a Routine: Incorporate daily or weekly practices for each pillar, such as mindfulness, self-reflection, or goal setting.

Seek Support: Seek guidance from mentors, therapists, or support groups to enhance your understanding and application of the pillars.

Celebrate Progress: Acknowledge your achievements and growth in each pillar, reinforcing your commitment.

Practice Patience: Understand that cultivating balanced self-esteem is a journey that requires patience and self-compassion.

In conclusion, cultivating a balanced and holistic self-esteem is a transformative practice that empowers you to develop a comprehensive sense of self-worth. By nurturing all six pillars of self-esteem, you create a strong foundation for authenticity, purposeful living, and meaningful connections with yourself and others. This approach contributes to enhanced well-being, resilience, and a more fulfilling and empowered life.

CHAPTER 4

PRACTICAL APPLICATIONS

Developing self-esteem in different life areas (work, relationships, etc.)

Developing self-esteem in different life areas, such as work, relationships, and personal pursuits, involves applying the principles of the six pillars of self-esteem to each specific context. By tailoring your practices to address the unique challenges and dynamics of each area, you can enhance your self-esteem, confidence, and overall well-being. Here's a detailed explanation of how to develop self-esteem in different life areas:

1. Work/Career:

Living Consciously: Approach your work with mindfulness, staying present in tasks and interactions to maximize productivity and satisfaction.

Self-Acceptance: Embrace your strengths and acknowledge areas for growth, allowing yourself to learn and improve without self-criticism.

Self-Responsibility: Take ownership of your tasks, decisions, and professional development, demonstrating accountability and initiative.

Living Purposefully: Set meaningful career goals that align with your values and passions, contributing to a sense of fulfillment.

Personal Integrity: Uphold ethical standards and honesty in your work interactions, building trust with colleagues and clients.

Building Trust/Credibility: Deliver consistent and high-quality work, earning the trust and respect of peers and superiors.

2. Relationships:

Living Consciously: Practice active listening and empathy, being fully present in conversations and nurturing deeper connections.

Self-Acceptance: Embrace your authentic self in relationships, allowing others to know and appreciate you for who you truly are.

Self-Responsibility: Take responsibility for your actions, emotions, and contributions to relationships, fostering open communication.

Living Purposefully: Cultivate relationships that align with your values and provide mutual support and growth.

Personal Integrity: Be honest and transparent in your interactions, maintaining trust and avoiding deception.

Building Trust/Credibility: Uphold your commitments and promises, demonstrating reliability and dependability to those close to you.

3. Personal Pursuits/Hobbies:

Living Consciously: Immerse yourself fully in your hobbies, engaging mindfully to derive maximum enjoyment and satisfaction.

Self-Acceptance: Embrace your unique interests and talents, appreciating your individuality without comparison to others.

Self-Responsibility: Set personal goals for your pursuits, holding yourself accountable for your progress and growth.

Living Purposefully: Pursue hobbies that bring you joy and align with your passions, contributing to a well-rounded life.

Personal Integrity: Approach your hobbies with integrity, respecting rules and guidelines while also respecting the environment and others.

Building Trust/Credibility: Participate actively in hobby communities, contributing positively and earning the trust of fellow enthusiasts.

4. Health and Well-Being:

Living Consciously: Practice mindful eating, exercise, and self-care to enhance your physical and mental well-being.

Self-Acceptance: Embrace your body and its uniqueness, valuing yourself regardless of external appearance.

Self-Responsibility: Take responsibility for your health by making informed choices, seeking medical care when needed, and setting wellness goals.

Living Purposefully: Cultivate healthy habits that align with your values and contribute to your overall vitality.

Personal Integrity: Be honest with yourself about your health behaviors, avoid self-deception, and commit to positive changes.

Building Trust/Credibility: Prioritize your health commitments and demonstrate consistency in self-care, building trust in your ability to maintain well-being.

By applying the principles of the six pillars of self-esteem to different life areas, you can develop a well-rounded and resilient self-esteem that empowers you to navigate various contexts with authenticity, purpose, and confidence.

Strategies for enhancing each pillar

1. Living Consciously:

Practice mindfulness meditation to cultivate present-moment awareness.

Engage in activities that bring you joy and make you feel fully alive.

Regularly reflect on your thoughts, feelings, and behaviors to increase self-awareness.

Limit multitasking and focus on one task at a time to promote mindful living.

2. Self-Acceptance:

Practice self-compassion by treating yourself with the same kindness you would offer a friend.

Challenge and reframe negative self-talk to promote a more positive self-image.

Engage in self-care routines that prioritize your well-being and demonstrate self-love.

Embrace your imperfections and view them as part of your unique identity.

3. Self-Responsibility:

Set clear goals and create action plans to achieve them, holding yourself accountable.

Make conscious choices based on your values, even in challenging situations.

Reflect on your decisions and their outcomes, learning from both successes and failures.

Take responsibility for your emotions by acknowledging them and finding healthy ways to express them.

4. Living Purposefully:

Identify your core values and align your goals and actions with them.

Break down larger goals into smaller, actionable steps to make progress over time.

Regularly assess your goals to ensure they continue to align with your evolving passions and aspirations.

Seek out opportunities for personal growth and learning that resonate with your sense of purpose.

5. Personal Integrity:

Make honesty a priority in your interactions, avoiding lies or exaggerations.

Practice transparency by openly sharing your thoughts and feelings with others.

Honor your commitments and promises, even when it requires extra effort or sacrifice.

Admit and learn from your mistakes, taking responsibility for any negative consequences.

6. Building Trust/Credibility:

Communicate clearly and consistently with others to establish reliable expectations.

Follow through on your commitments and deliver on promises, earning trust over time.

Be a good listener, demonstrating respect for others' perspectives and opinions.

Act ethically and avoid actions that could damage your reputation or credibility.

By intentionally applying these strategies to each of the six pillars of self-esteem, you can foster personal growth, enhance your self-esteem, and create a foundation for a more fulfilling and empowered life.

CHAPTER 5

OVERCOMING CHALLENGES

Common obstacles to building self-esteem

Building self-esteem can be a rewarding journey, but it's not without its challenges. Several common obstacles can hinder the development of healthy self-esteem. Recognizing and addressing these obstacles is essential for personal growth and well-being. Here's a detailed explanation of some common obstacles to building self-esteem:

Negative Self-Talk and Self-Criticism:

Explanation: Constantly berating yourself with negative thoughts and self-criticism can erode self-esteem over time.
Solution: Practice self-compassion and challenge negative self-talk by countering it with positive affirmations and realistic perspectives.
Perfectionism:

Explanation: Striving for perfection can lead to chronic dissatisfaction and fear of failure, undermining self-esteem.
Solution: Embrace a growth mindset, acknowledge mistakes as learning opportunities, and focus on progress rather than perfection.

Comparison and Social Comparison Bias:

Explanation: Comparing yourself to others, especially on social media, can lead to feelings of inadequacy and lower self-esteem.
Solution: Cultivate self-awareness, recognize your unique qualities, and limit exposure to unhealthy comparisons.
Lack of Self-Acceptance:

Explanation: Difficulty accepting yourself as you are can lead to a constant sense of dissatisfaction.
Solution: Practice self-compassion, challenge unrealistic standards, and focus on your strengths and positive qualities.
Fear of Rejection and Criticism:

Explanation: The fear of being rejected or criticized can prevent you from expressing yourself authentically.
Solution: Gradually expose yourself to situations that challenge this fear, seeking supportive environments for self-expression.
Past Trauma or Negative Experiences:

Explanation: Previous traumas or negative experiences can contribute to feelings of unworthiness and low self-esteem.
Solution: Consider seeking therapy or counseling to address and heal from past wounds, enabling you to build a healthier self-image.

External Validation Dependency:

Explanation: Relying solely on external validation for self-worth can lead to insecurity when that validation is absent.

Solution: Cultivate self-validation by recognizing your achievements and inner qualities, regardless of external opinions.

Lack of Boundaries:

Explanation: Not setting and enforcing personal boundaries can lead to feelings of being taken advantage of, undermining self-esteem.

Solution: Learn to communicate assertively and establish healthy boundaries in relationships and situations.

Stagnation and Lack of Goals:

Explanation: A lack of purpose and meaningful goals can contribute to a sense of aimlessness and diminished self-esteem.

Solution: Set achievable goals that align with your values, providing a sense of direction and accomplishment.

Cultural and Societal Pressures:

Explanation: Societal standards and expectations can create unrealistic ideals that impact self-esteem.

Solution: Develop a critical perspective on cultural influences and focus on values that align with your authentic self.

By addressing these obstacles and employing strategies to overcome them, you can cultivate a stronger sense of self-esteem and embark on a journey of personal growth, self-acceptance, and empowerment.

Techniques for overcoming self-doubt and setbacks

Overcoming self-doubt and setbacks is essential for building and maintaining a healthy self-esteem. These challenges are common and can hinder personal growth and well-being. Employing effective techniques can help you navigate through self-doubt and setbacks, ultimately strengthening your self-esteem. Here's a detailed explanation of techniques to overcome self-doubt and setbacks:

1. Practice Self-Compassion:

Explanation: Treat yourself with the same kindness and understanding you would offer to a friend facing difficulties. How to Use: When self-doubt arises, remind yourself that everyone experiences setbacks. Speak to yourself with self-compassionate language and acknowledge that making mistakes is a part of learning and growth.

2. Challenge Negative Thoughts:

Explanation: Negative thoughts contribute to self-doubt. Challenge and reframe these thoughts to create a more balanced perspective.

How to Use: When self-doubt arises, identify the negative thought patterns and counter them with evidence of your achievements, strengths, and past successes.

3. Set Realistic Goals:

Explanation: Setting overly ambitious goals can lead to feelings of failure. Setting realistic goals promotes a sense of accomplishment.

How to Use: Break down larger goals into smaller, achievable steps. Celebrate each step you complete, reinforcing a positive self-image.

4. Practice Resilience:

Explanation: Resilience helps you bounce back from setbacks. Developing this trait strengthens your ability to overcome challenges.

How to Use: View setbacks as opportunities for growth. Focus on your capacity to adapt and learn from difficult situations.

5. Seek Support:

Explanation: Connect with friends, family, or a therapist who can provide encouragement, perspective, and validation.
How to Use: When self-doubt is overwhelming or setbacks feel insurmountable, reach out to your support network for guidance and reassurance.

6. Visualize Success:

Explanation: Visualization can help you build confidence and reduce self-doubt by mentally rehearsing successful outcomes.
How to Use: Visualize yourself overcoming challenges and achieving your goals. Engage your senses and emotions to make the visualization more vivid.

7. Embrace Growth Mindset:

Explanation: Adopt a growth mindset, understanding that setbacks are opportunities for learning and improvement.
How to Use: Instead of viewing setbacks as failures, see them as valuable experiences that contribute to your personal development.

8. Focus on Strengths:

Explanation: Acknowledge and leverage your strengths to counter feelings of self-doubt.

How to Use: Create a list of your strengths and refer to it when self-doubt arises. Remind yourself of your capabilities and accomplishments.

9. Celebrate Small Wins:

Explanation: Celebrating even small achievements boosts your self-esteem and provides motivation to overcome self-doubt.

How to Use: Recognize and reward yourself for each step you take toward your goals, reinforcing your sense of accomplishment.

10. Learn from Setbacks:

- Explanation: Viewing setbacks as learning opportunities helps you gain insights and prevent future mistakes.
- How to Use: Reflect on what went wrong and what you can learn from the setback. Use this knowledge to adjust your approach and move forward.

By incorporating these techniques into your daily life, you can effectively navigate through self-doubt and setbacks, building resilience, confidence, and a healthier self-esteem. Remember that overcoming these challenges is a gradual process, and consistent effort will lead to greater self-assurance and personal growth.

Encouragement for continued self-improvement

Continued self-improvement is a lifelong journey that holds the potential for personal growth, fulfillment, and an enhanced sense of self-esteem. While the path may have its ups and downs, the rewards of your efforts can be truly transformative. Here's a detailed explanation of encouragement to fuel your ongoing self-improvement:

1. Embrace Progress Over Perfection:

Understand that self-improvement is about growth, not achieving a state of perfection.
Celebrate even the smallest steps forward, as they contribute to your overall progress.
Remember that setbacks and challenges are natural and provide opportunities to learn and refine your approach.

2. Cultivate Self-Compassion:

Treat yourself with kindness and understanding, especially during times of struggle.

Recognize that everyone faces obstacles on their journey of self-improvement.

Practice self-compassion by speaking to yourself as you would to a supportive friend.

3. Focus on Personal Growth, Not Comparison:

Avoid comparing your journey to others', as each person's path is unique.

Measure your progress against your own goals and aspirations, rather than external standards.

Appreciate the individuality of your journey and the lessons it brings.

4. Embrace the Power of Persistence:

Understand that significant change takes time and consistent effort.

Stay committed to your goals even when progress seems slow or obstacles arise.

Each step you take brings you closer to your desired outcomes.

5. Reflect on How Far You've Come:

Periodically review your journey and acknowledge the growth you've achieved.
Recognize the challenges you've overcome and the skills you've developed.
Use your past successes as motivation to continue pushing forward.

6. Embrace Lifelong Learning:

Approach each day with curiosity and a willingness to learn something new.
Pursue knowledge and skills that align with your interests and aspirations.
Embrace challenges as opportunities to expand your horizons and develop new abilities.

7. Set Meaningful Goals:

Define clear, specific, and achievable goals that resonate with your values.
Break down larger goals into smaller, manageable steps to maintain focus and motivation.

Establish a sense of purpose by aligning your goals with your passions and ambitions.

8. Seek Support and Accountability:

Surround yourself with a supportive network of friends, mentors, or coaches.
Share your goals and progress with others who can provide encouragement and guidance.
Accountability partners can help you stay on track and motivated.

9. Embrace Resilience and Adaptability:

View challenges as opportunities to develop resilience and adaptability.
Embrace setbacks as learning experiences that contribute to your overall growth.
Reframe adversity as a chance to test your skills and determination.

10. Cultivate a Positive Mindset:
- Foster a positive outlook by focusing on what you've achieved and what you can accomplish.
- Challenge negative thoughts with constructive self-talk and affirmations.

- Believe in your ability to create positive change in your life.

Remember that self-improvement is not a destination but an ongoing journey filled with opportunities for growth, discovery, and self-fulfillment. By approaching this journey with patience, self-compassion, and a willingness to learn, you can create a more empowered and meaningful life for yourself.

CONCLUSION

In conclusion, the pursuit of self-esteem is a multifaceted journey that encompasses the development and cultivation of six fundamental pillars: Living Consciously, Self-Acceptance, Self-Responsibility, Living Purposefully, Personal Integrity, and Building Trust/Credibility. These pillars form the cornerstone of a healthy and empowered sense of self-worth, contributing to personal growth, resilience, and overall well-being.

Throughout this discussion, we've explored each pillar in depth, understanding their significance and practical applications. Living Consciously involves self-awareness and mindfulness, while Self-Acceptance encourages embracing both strengths and weaknesses. Self-Responsibility emphasizes accountability, and

Living Purposefully underscores the importance of setting and pursuing meaningful goals. Personal Integrity stresses honesty, and Building Trust/Credibility focuses on building trustworthy relationships.

Moreover, we've discussed how these pillars interact and reinforce one another, creating a harmonious cycle of self-improvement and empowerment. The interconnected nature of the pillars highlights the importance of nurturing all aspects of self-esteem for a balanced and holistic sense of self-worth.

We've also addressed common obstacles that can impede the development of self-esteem and provided techniques to overcome self-doubt and setbacks. By cultivating self-compassion, challenging negative thoughts, and seeking support, individuals can navigate challenges and setbacks with resilience and a positive mindset.

The journey of self-improvement is not linear; it is marked by progress, setbacks, and ongoing growth. By embracing self-compassion, setting meaningful goals, and fostering a growth mindset, individuals can embark on a lifelong journey of personal development that leads to enhanced self-esteem, increased self-confidence, and a more fulfilling and empowered life.

Ultimately, the pursuit of self-esteem is a testament to your commitment to self-discovery, self-acceptance, and continual self-improvement. By integrating the principles discussed here into your daily life, you can build a strong foundation for a healthier, more authentic, and more fulfilling sense of self-esteem. Embrace the challenges and triumphs, and remember that every step you take contributes to your journey toward a more empowered and meaningful existence.

Made in United States
Troutdale, OR
01/31/2024